RETRO

NOMADS

retro1

/ˈrɛtrəʊ/

Learn to pronounce

adjective

adjective: **retro**

1. 1.
imitative of a style or fashion from the recent past.
"retro 60s fashions"

synonyms:

in period style, period, nostalgic, evocative, of
yesteryear, olde worlde;
dated, old-fashioned, backward-looking, retrogressive,
out of date, passé
"a retro restaurant with a Fifties-style lunch counter"

noun

noun: **retro**

1. 1.
retro clothes, music, or style.
"a look which mixes Italian casual wear and American
retro"

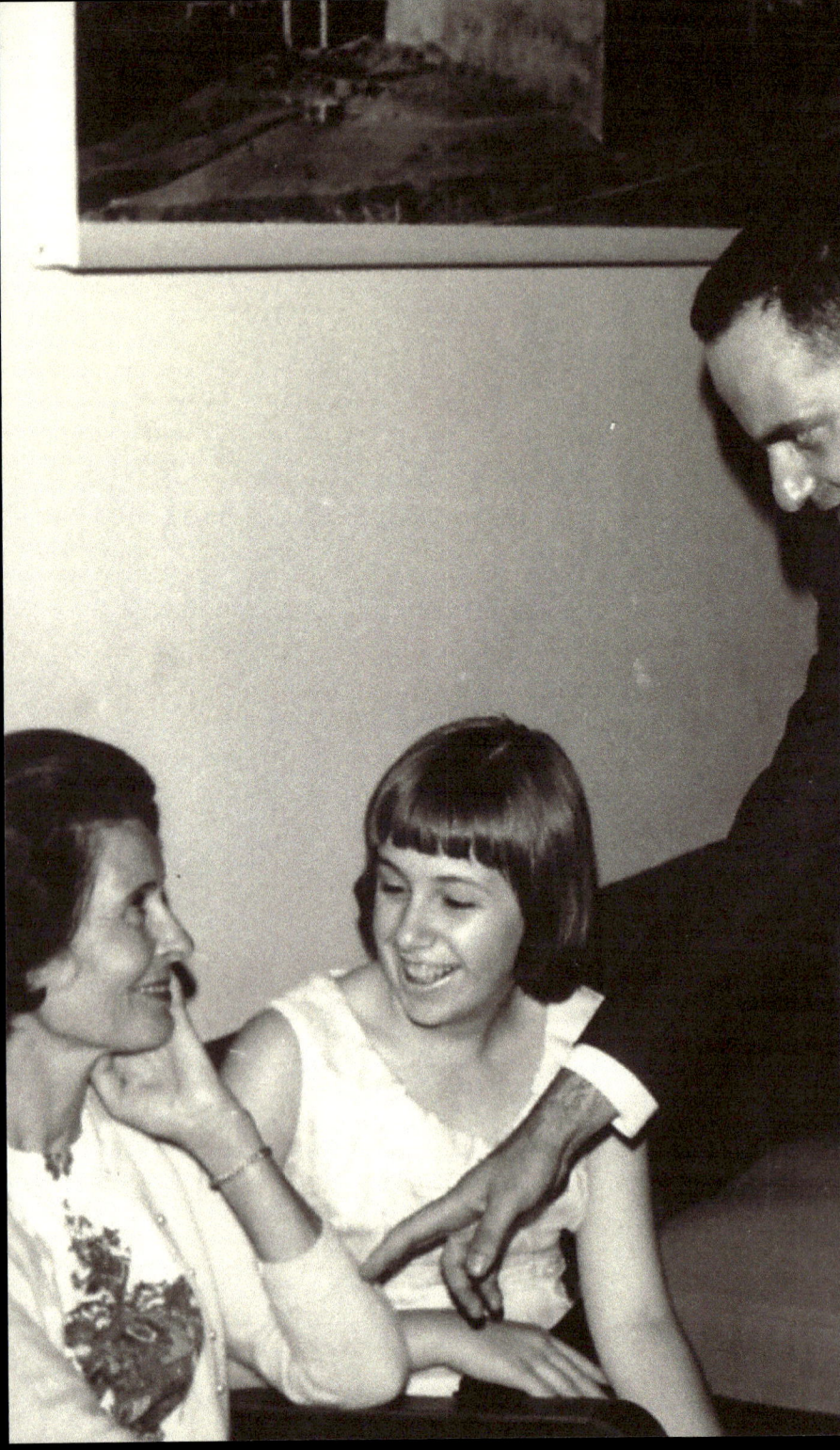

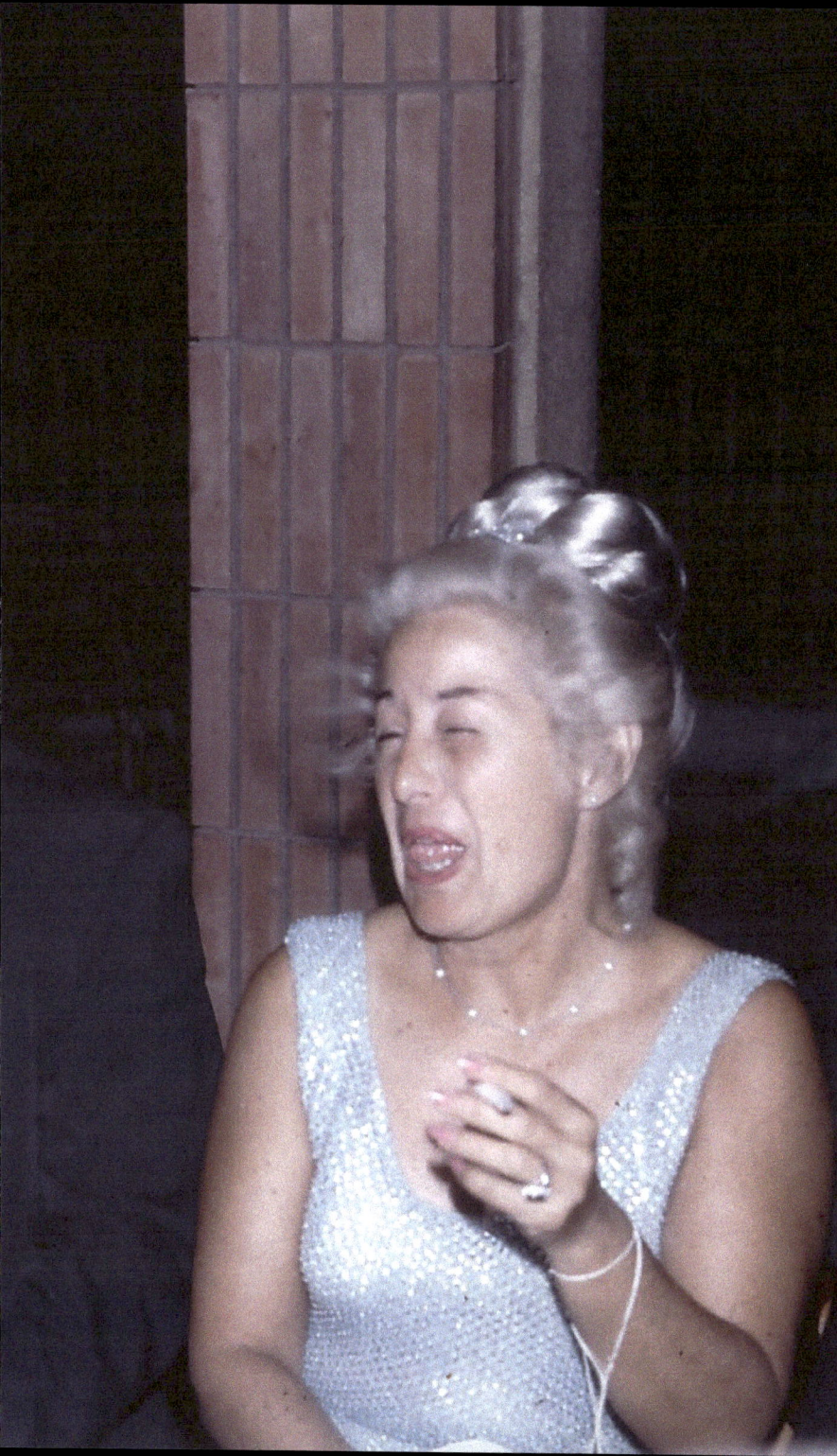

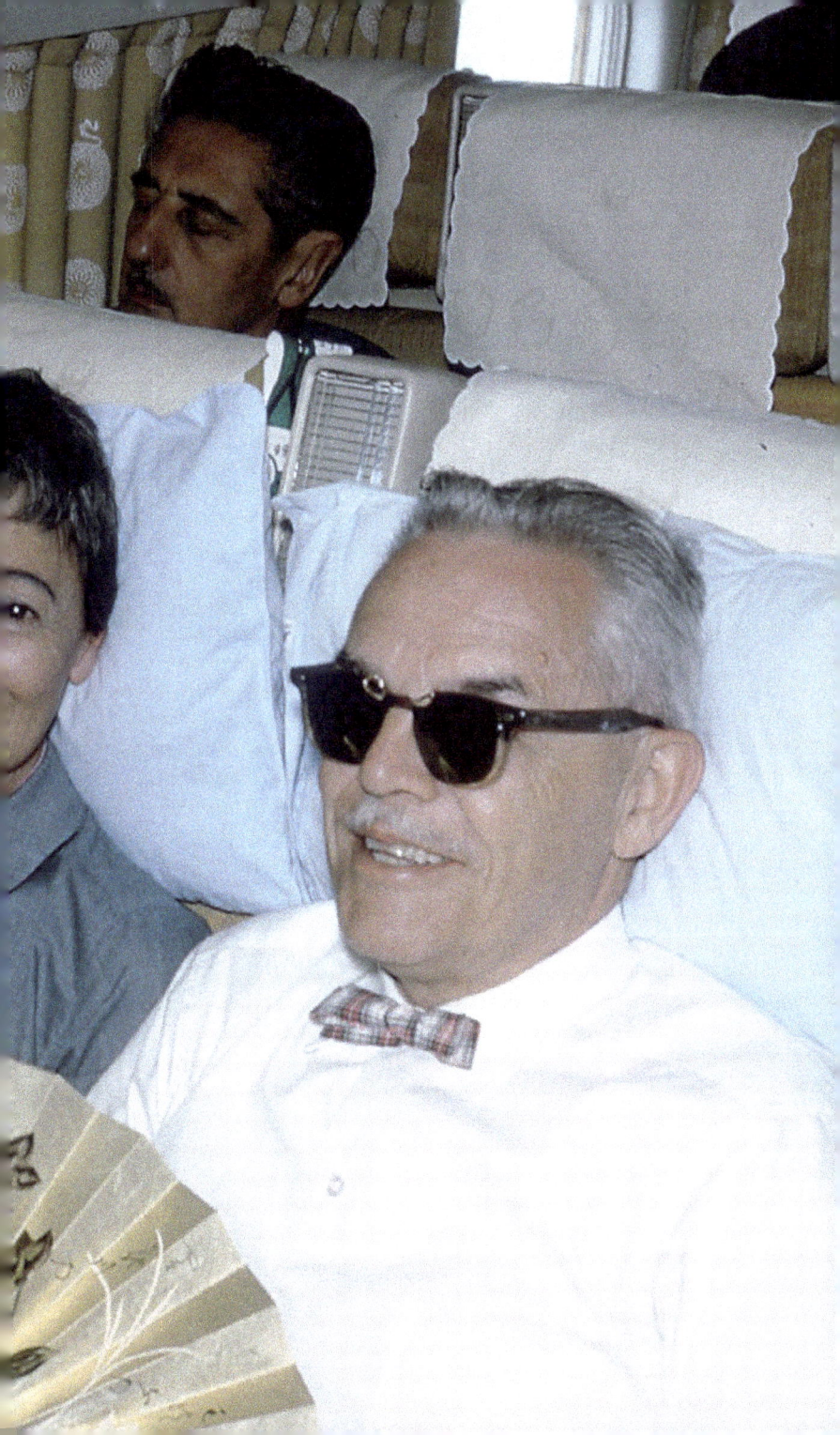

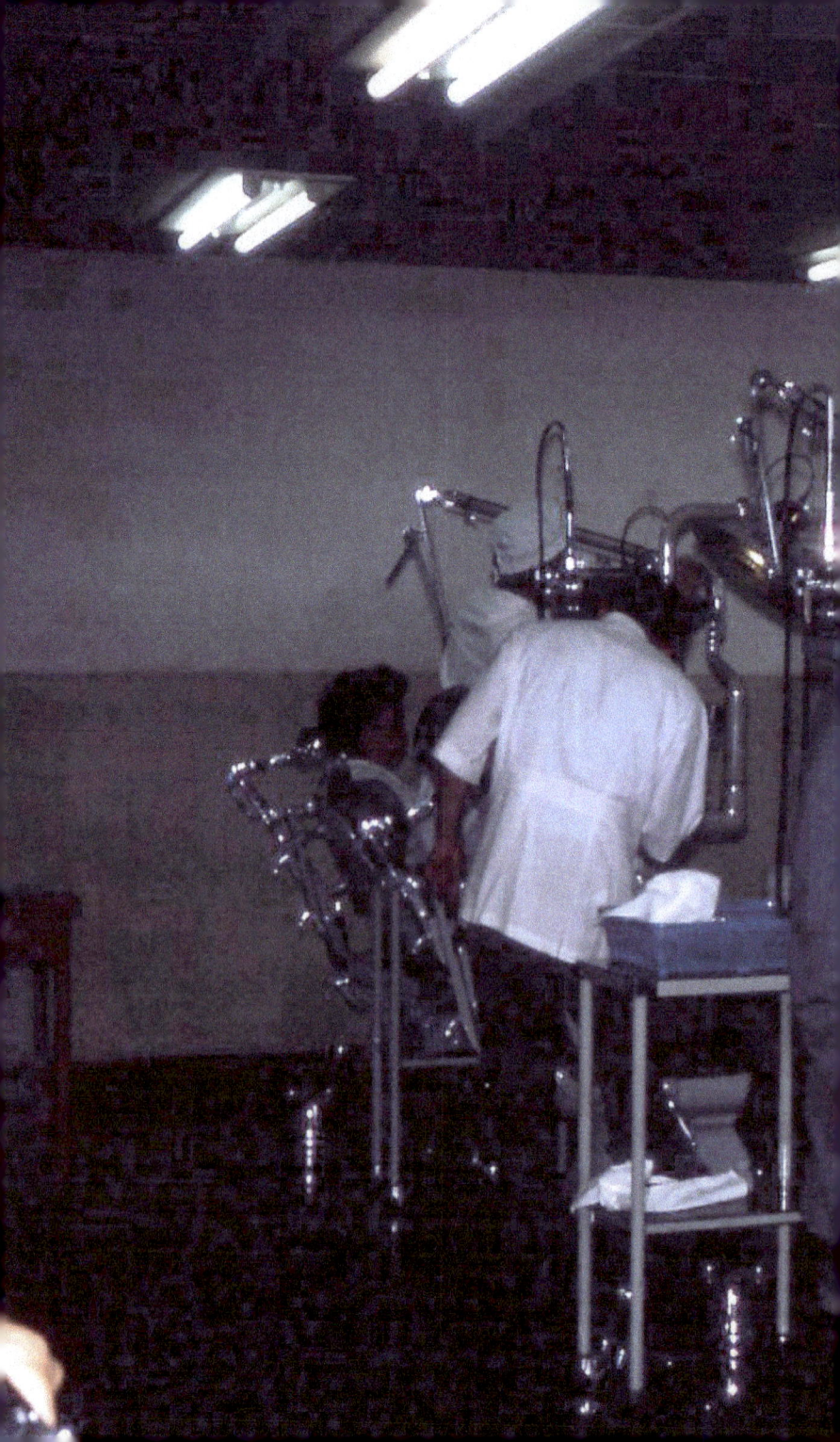

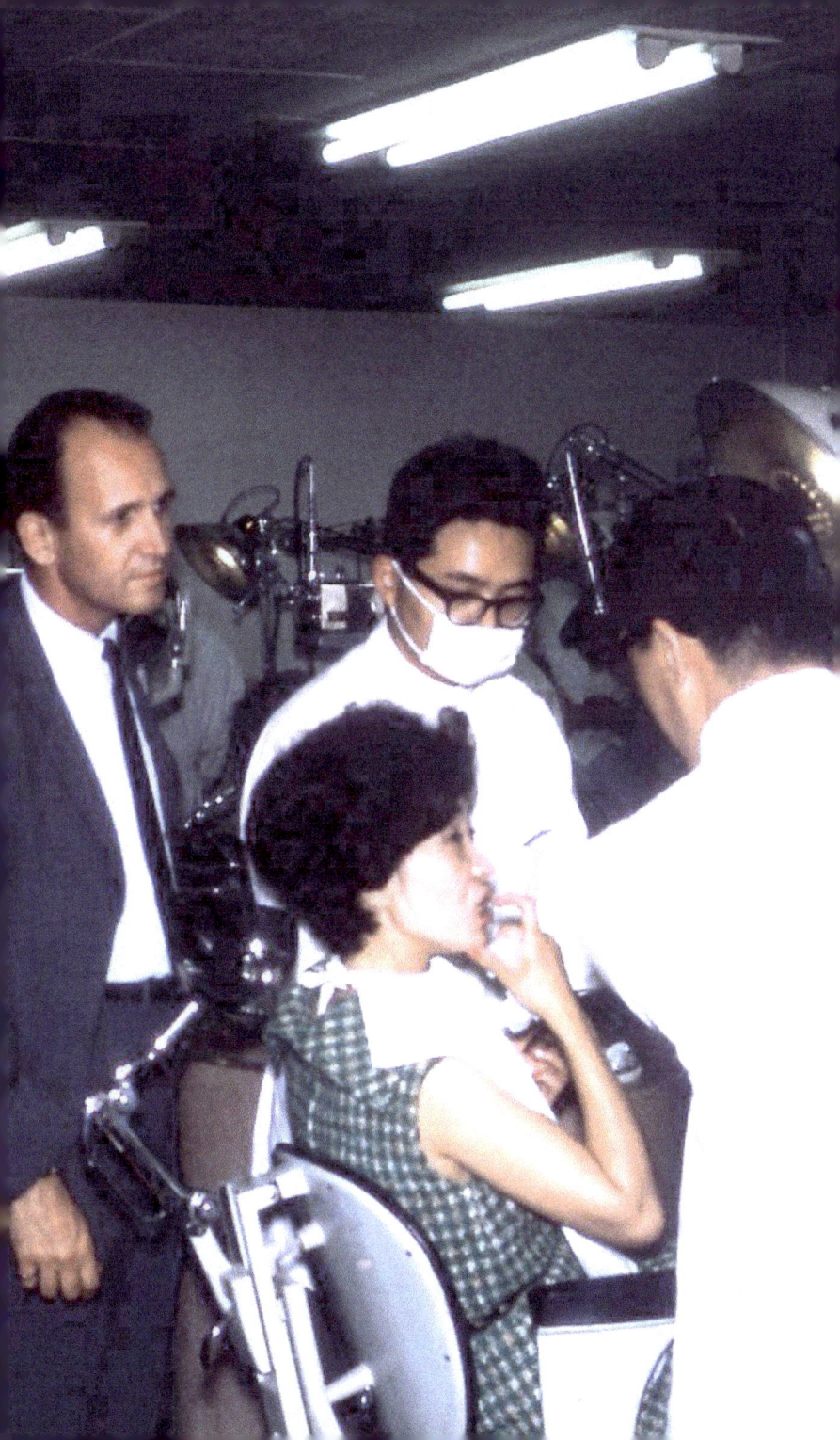

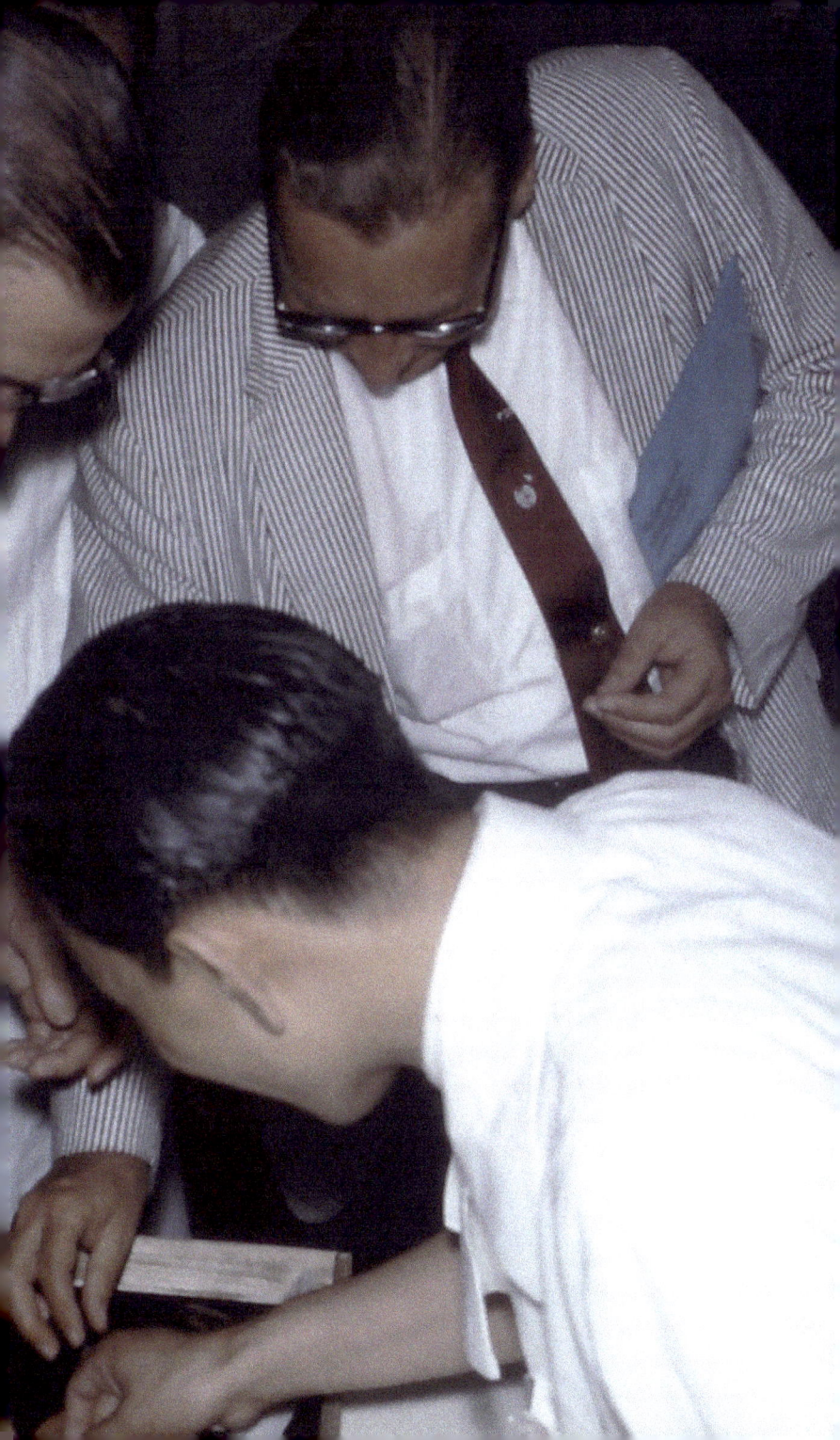

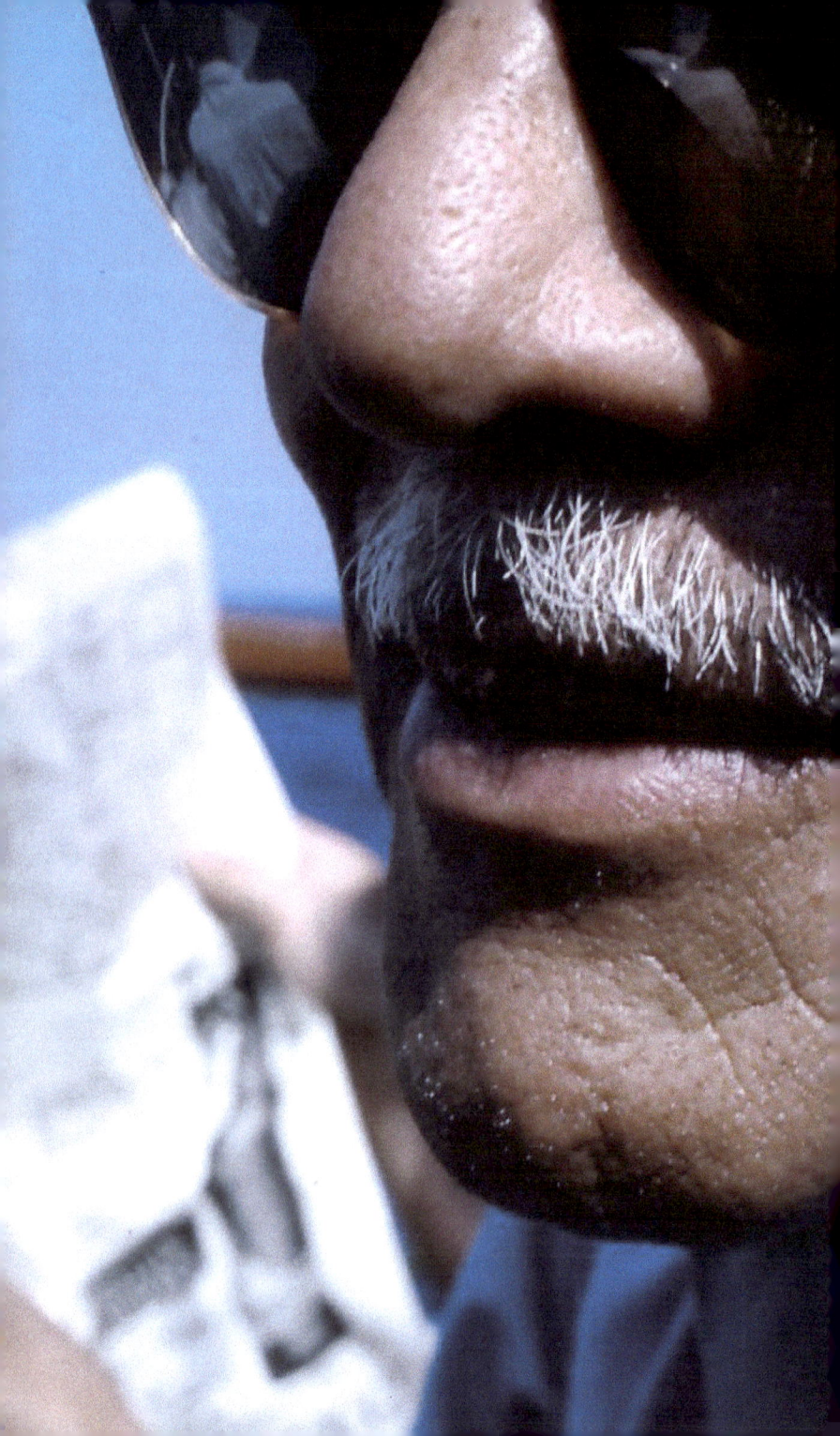

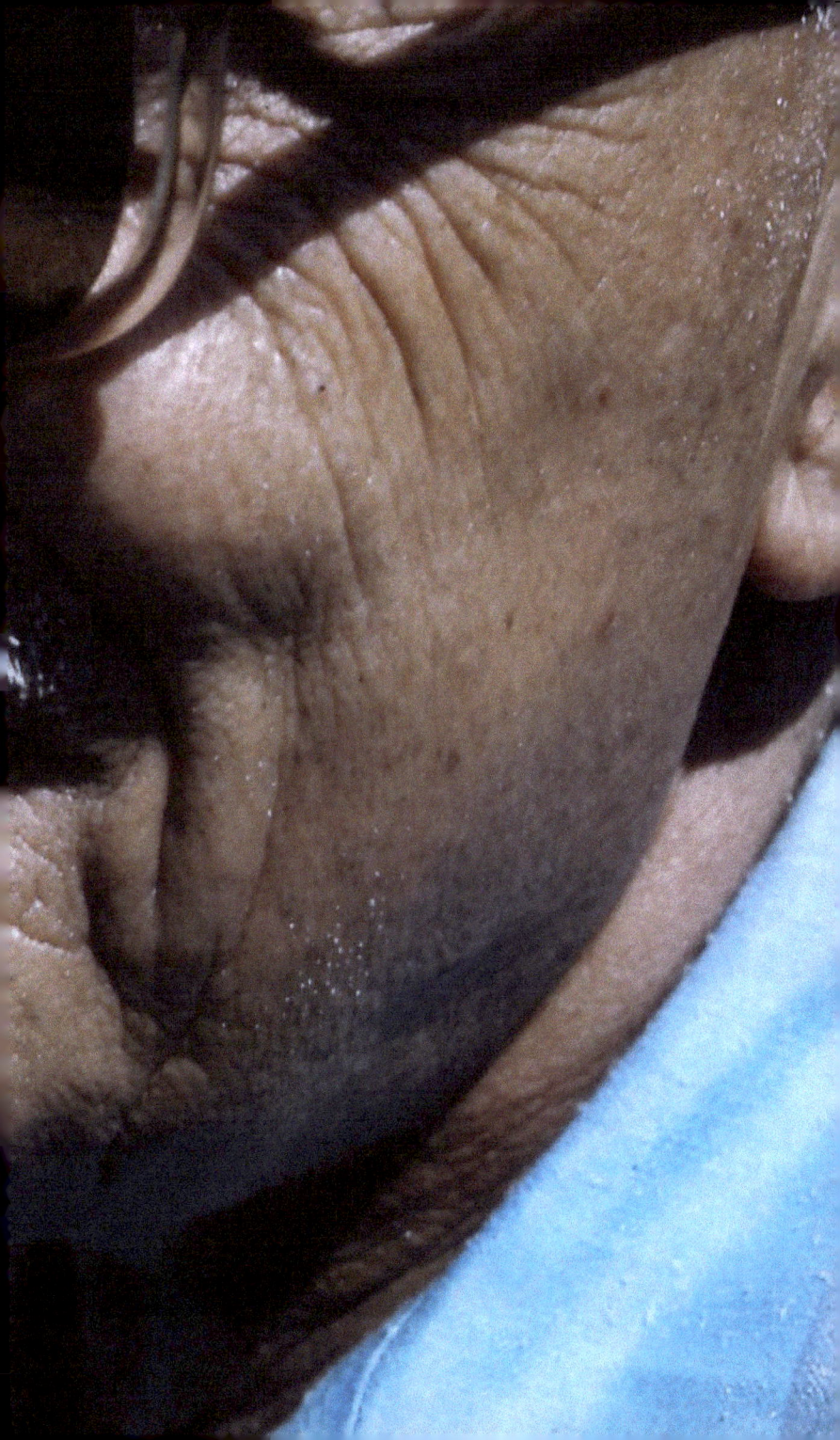

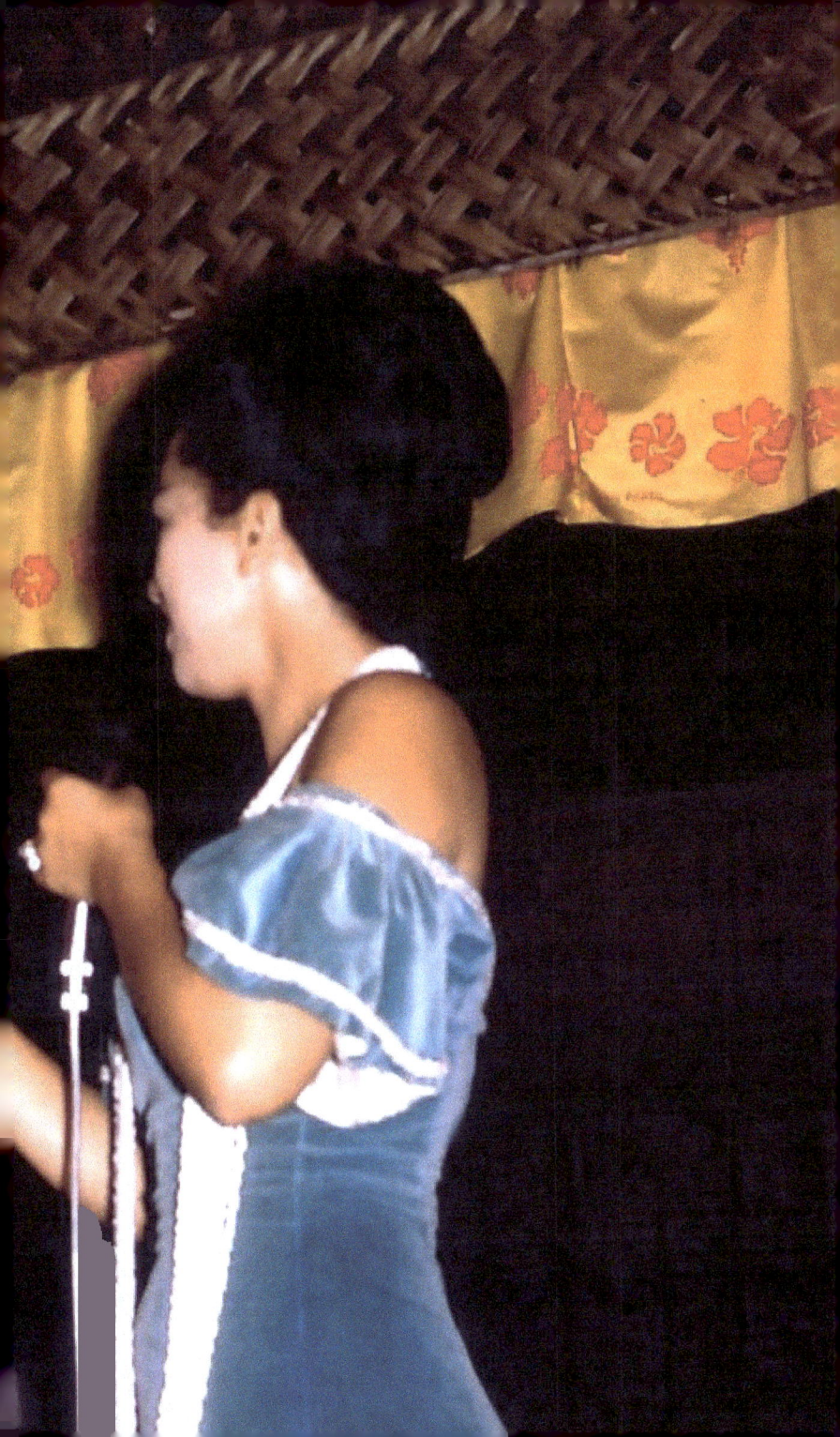

PORTUGAL

1434
C. BOJADOR
1441

1444
CABO VERDE

GUINE
1460

147
MINA

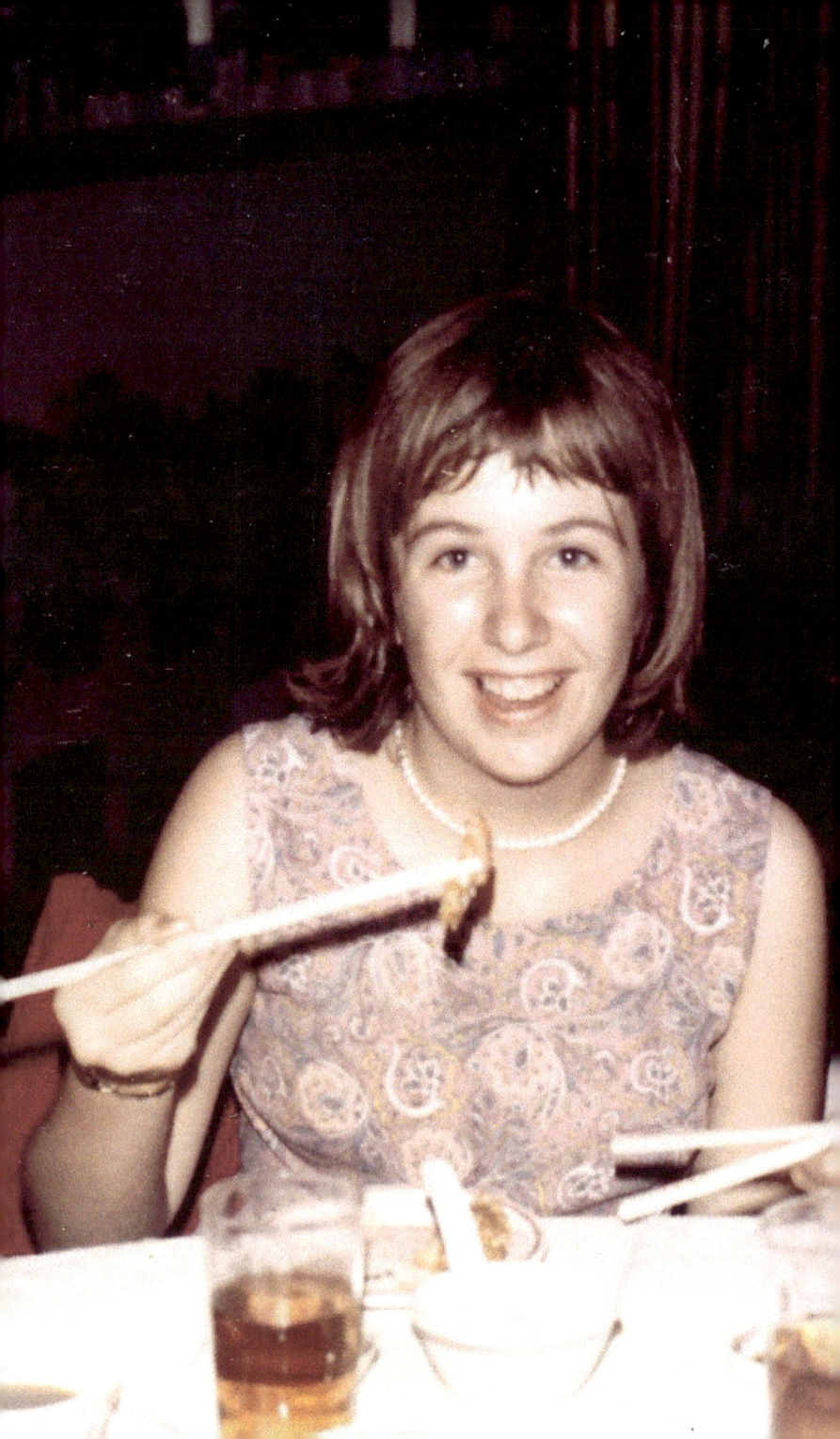

新聞盛

WELCOME TO

HONG KONG

Wonderful
World of
Dentistry Tour

WONDERFUL
WORLD OF
DENTISTRY TOUR

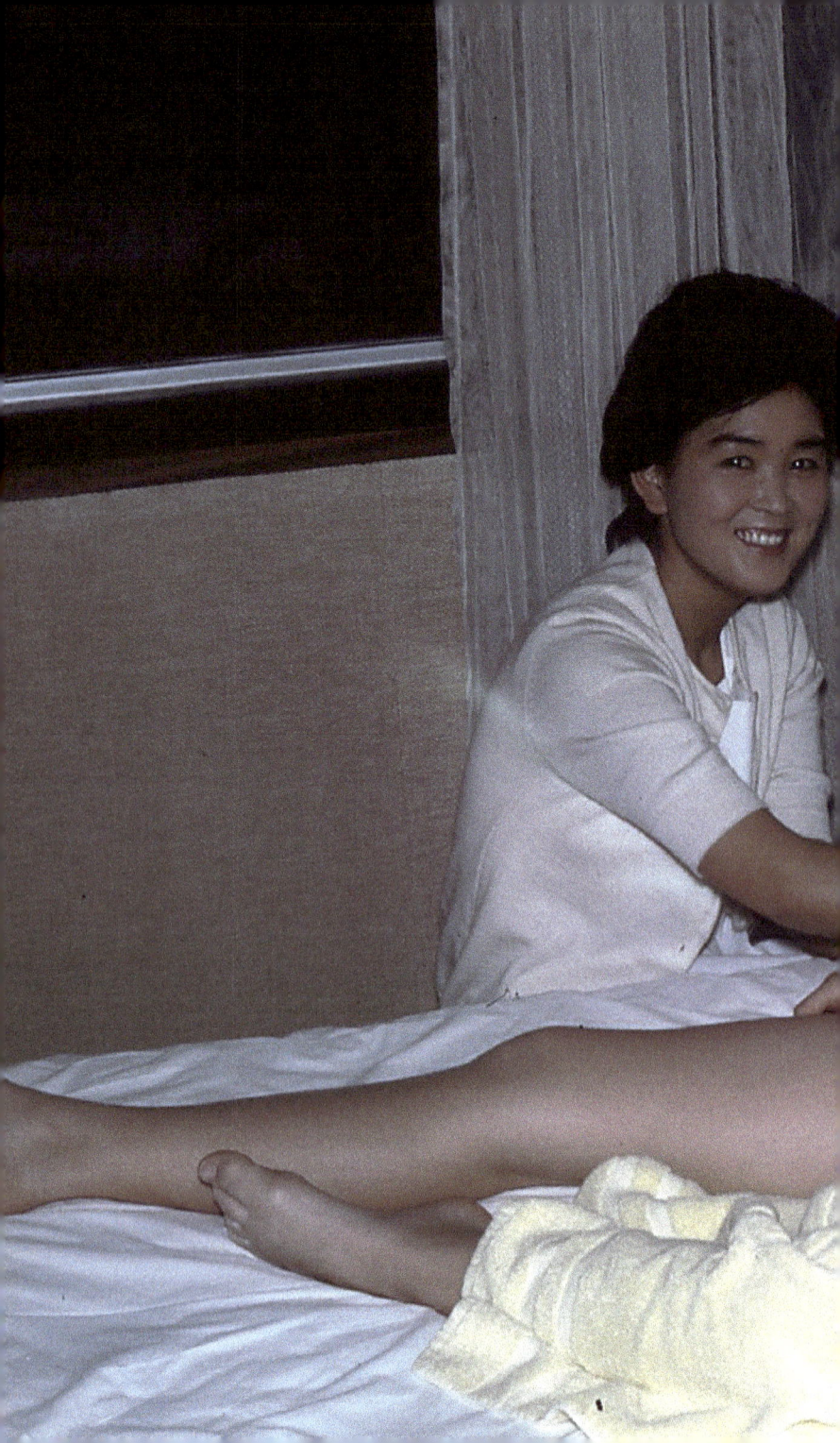

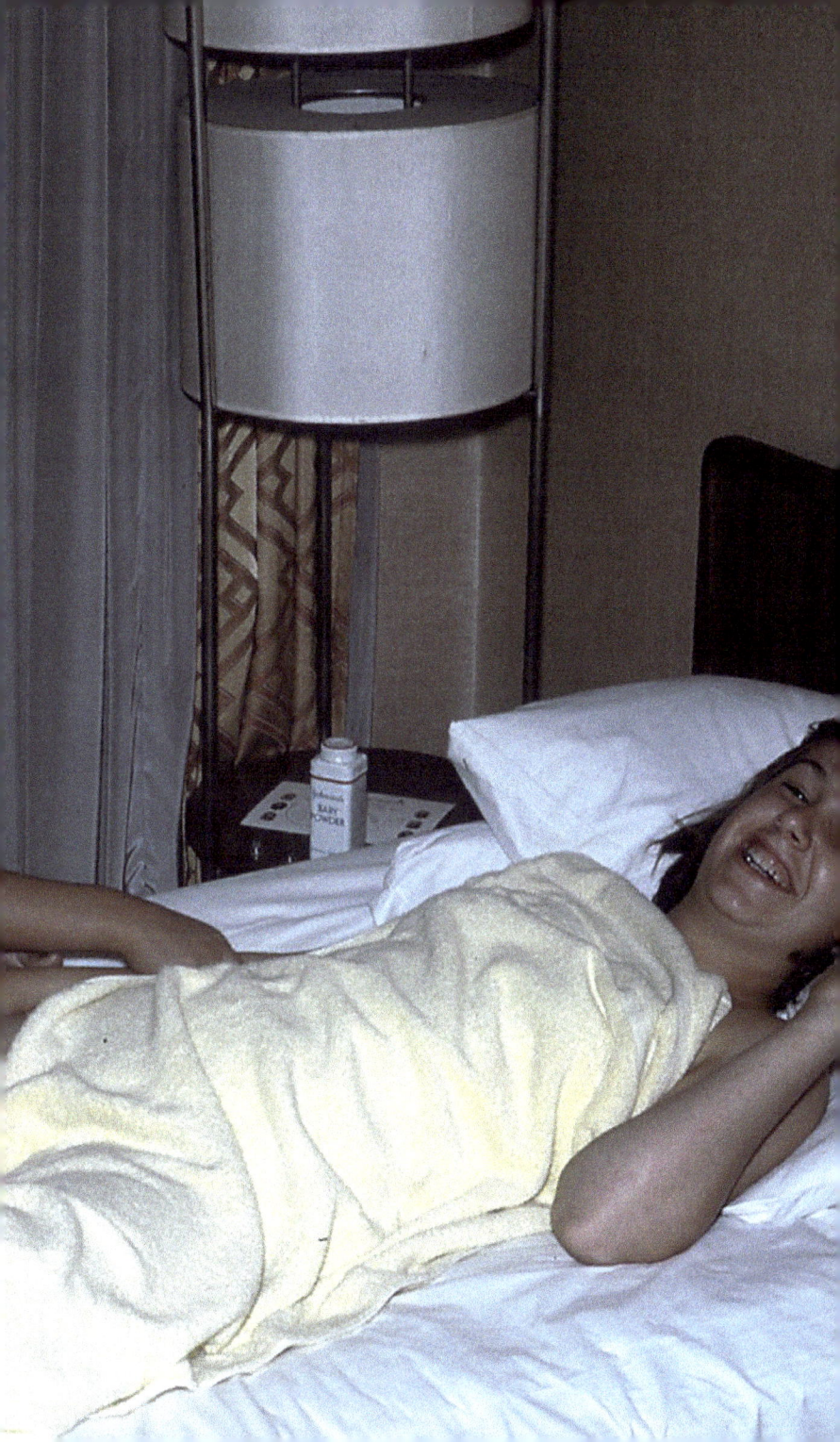

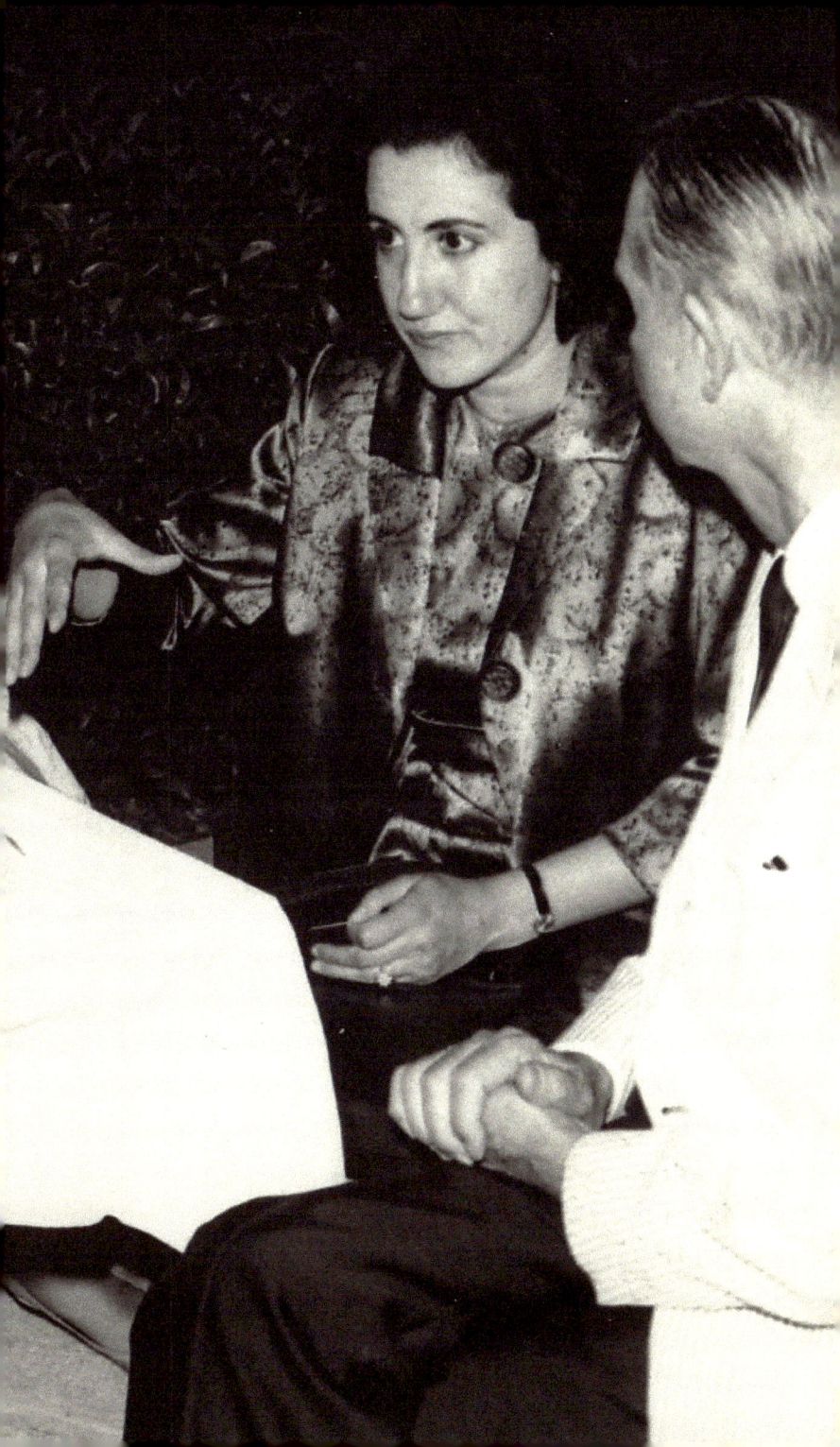

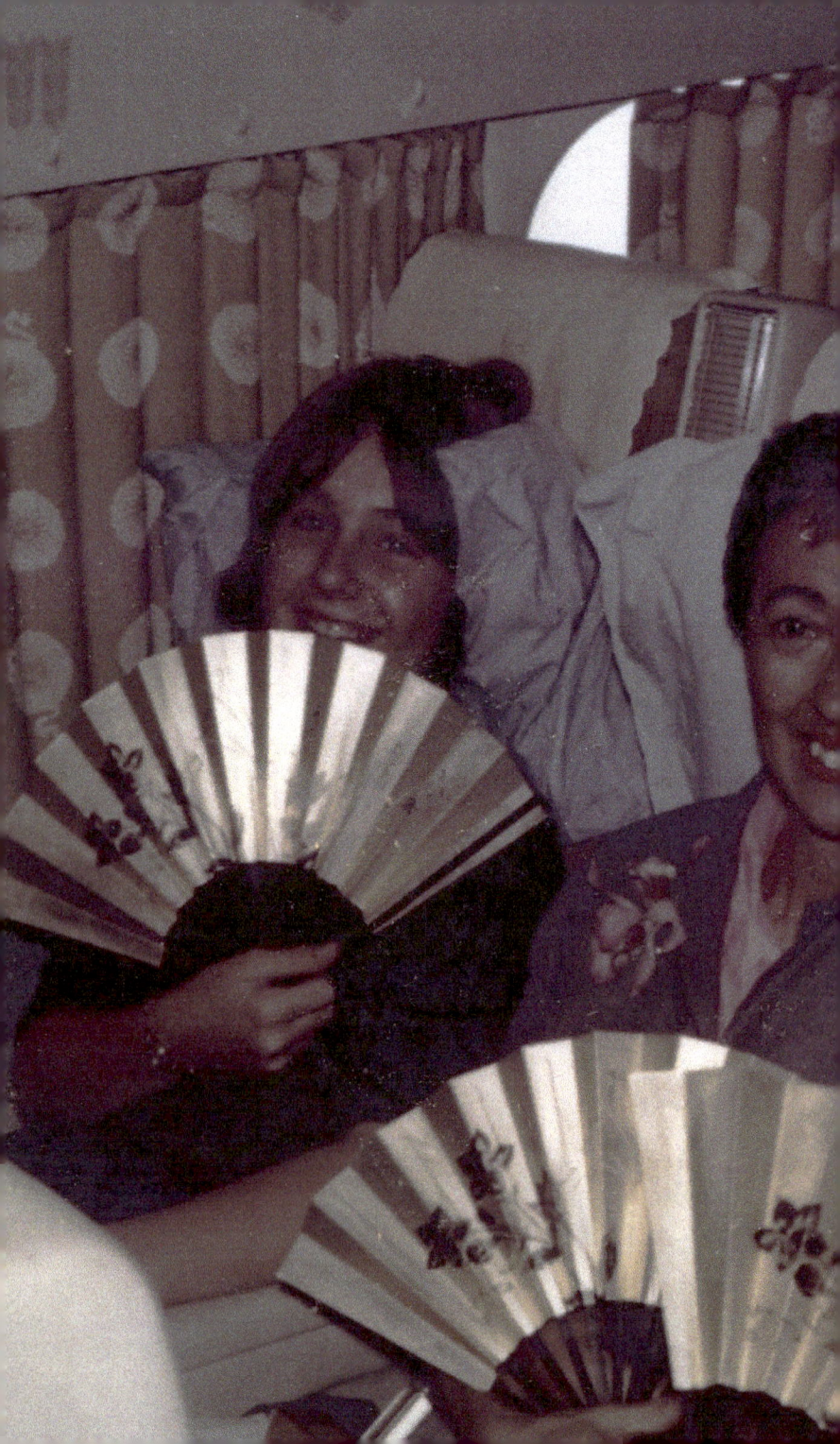

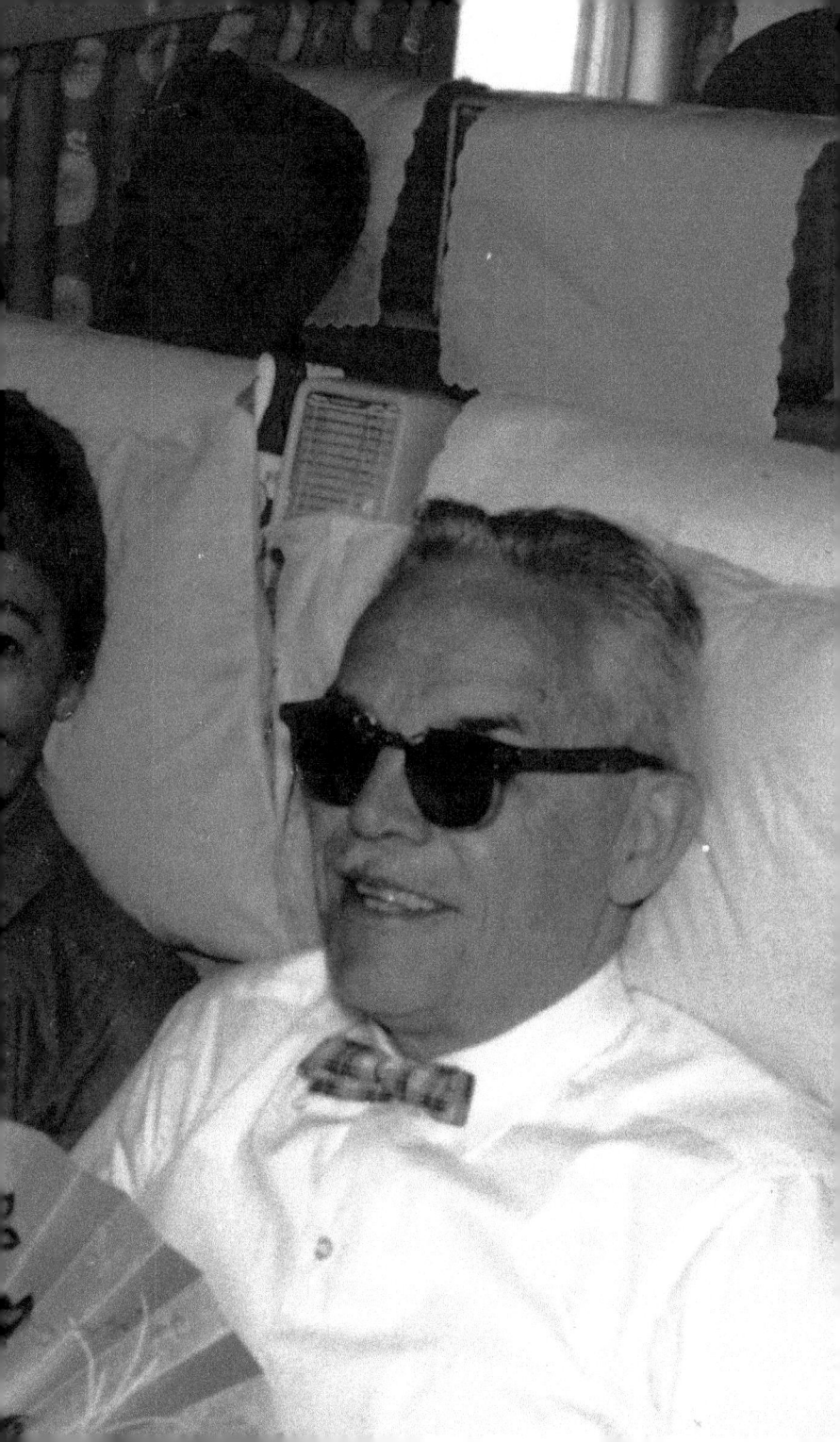

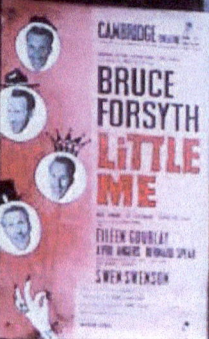

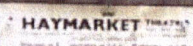

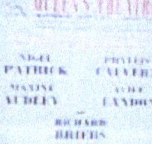

REDWOOD SEQUOIA SEMPERVIRENS
WASHED ASHORE AT CRESCENT CITY
DURING THE CHRISTMAS FLOOD OF
1964. PLACED HERE AT THE GATEWAY
TO THE REDWOOD EMPIRE.
• MAY 10, 1965 •

SHRI LAKSHMI NARA

BUILT 1938 A.D. 189

THIS TEMPLE IS BUILT FOR SHRI SANATAN DHARAM S

RAJA BALDEV DASS BIRLA. ALL HINDUS VA ALL B

DHARAM INCLUDING ARYA, BAUDH, JAIN SIKH M

WORSHIP, SATSANG AND KIRTAN IN CONSONANCE W

TEMPLE IN MUTUAL HARMONY AND GOOD WILL.

THIS TEMPLE IS OPEN TO ALL HINDUS INCLUDIN

PRESCRIBED CONDITIONS OF CLEANLINESS, FULL FA

PERSONS SUFFERING FROM INFECTIOUS DISEAS

ALLOWED IN OR NEAR THE TEMPLE.

.NOTE: NONE BUT THE MANAGEMENT SHALL INTER

WHICH SHALL BE CONDUCTED ACCORDING TO SANATA

.MPLE

W DELHI BY SHRI SETH
OF SHRI SANATAN
CIPATE IN THE DAILY
ONVENTIONS OF THE

N SUBJECT TO THE
INCERE DEVOTION.
EGGARS ARE NOT

HE WORSHIP OF THE TEMPLE
RITES AND OBSVENANCES

CPSIA information can be obtained
at www.ICGtesting.com
Printed in the USA
BVHW090828290719
554567BV00025B/1930/P